Motorcycle Crashes

What You Need to Know If You are Injured

and What You Can Do about It

Slater & Zurz LLP

Attorneys at Law

Akron • Canton • Cleveland • Columbus

Motorcycle Crashes in Ohio

By: Slater & Zurz LLP

Attorneys at Law

Printed in the United States of America

First Printing 2015

For permission to reproduce or to order additional copies of this book, contact Slater & Zurz LLP by calling 1-800-297-9191 or visit our websites:

slaterzurz.com

ohiomotorcyclelaw.com

TABLE OF CONTENTS

Introduction

Most motorcyclists understand that the freedom and enjoyment they experience while riding comes with risk – risk of serious or fatal injury resulting from another motorist's carelessness. Motorcycles provide riders with little protection, as compared to cars and trucks, so injuries associated with motorcycle crashes tend to be more severe. That is true even for motorcyclists who obey traffic laws and take proper safety precautions. Motorcyclists cannot control the actions of other drivers on the road.

While motorcyclists have the same rights as other motorists, some people stereotype them as aggressive risk-takers and daredevils. For example, some view motorcyclists as people who often speed and pass cars in no-passing zones. Others believe the act of riding a motorcycle is, in and of itself, reckless. Others blame motorcyclists for assuming the risk of serious injury by not wearing a helmet. These prejudices can lead to unfair assumptions about who was at fault for the crash and the injuries involved.

One all too common claim that drivers make after a collision with a motorcycle is, "He came out of nowhere." While motorcycles may have a relatively narrow visual profile compared to larger vehicles, that does not automatically make the motorcyclist at fault for the crash.

This book is meant to provide motorcyclists and their families with some basic information about the prevalence of motorcycle crashes in Ohio, Ohio motorcycle safety laws, common causes of motorcycle crashes, motorcycle safety precautions, and a motorcyclist's legal rights if he or she is injured due to another motorist's carelessness.

Unfortunately, motorcycle crashes can disrupt the course of lives, sometimes forever. They can result in injuries that burden families with significant medical bills and deprive victims of their ability to work as they once did. Things become even more complicated when a victim's health insurance company demands to be re-paid for its payment of accident-related medical bills out of the injured person's legal claim.

Motorcyclists harmed by another's negligence have the right to seek compensation to help them and their families cope with the difficult road ahead, and they have the right to be treated fairly. Slater & Zurz LLP has the resources, skill, and knowledge to help you protect your rights.

For more than 40 years, Slater & Zurz LLP has been helping victims who have been wronged and injured by others. The firm will take aggressive action against any insurance company that tries to minimize payment or outright deny rightful compensation to its clients.

Slater & Zurz LLP offers free initial consultations. If the firm accepts your case, it will be done on a contingency fee basis. This means the firm will receive a portion of any award or settlement obtained on your behalf. If there is no recovery, you will not owe any fee.

Slater & Zurz LLP

Akron • Canton • Cleveland • Columbus

Call us for a free consultation with an experienced attorney:

1-800-297-9191

slaterzurz.com

ohiomotorcyclelaw.com

DISCLAIMER

The information contained within this book is for <u>informational use only</u>.

This book is not intended to be used as legal advice. No attorney-client relationship has been created or formed as a result of your receiving, purchasing, or reading this book.

Cases involving motorcycle crashes are unique, complex, and involve many different legal issues. The outcome of the case is dependent on the particulars of that specific case.

You should consult with a qualified Ohio attorney who is licensed and who has experience with motorcycle crash cases in the state of Ohio.

If you would like a free consultation with an attorney at the Ohio law firm of Slater & Zurz LLP, please call us at 1-800-297-9191 or visit slaterzurz.com and send a message from our website.

Chapter 1

Statistics about Ohio Motorcycle Crashes

According to statistical data compiled by the Ohio Department of Public Safety, there were 3,651 Ohio motorcycle crashes in 2014. These crashes resulted in 3,060 injuries and 140 deaths.

The data show that slightly more than 50 percent of those who suffered injury, or 1,550 riders, were not wearing a helmet. On the other hand, injured people wearing a helmet totaled 1,327. Approximately 26 percent of those killed in motorcycle crashes, or 37 people, were wearing a helmet, and 49.4 percent, or 91 people, were not wearing a helmet. It is unknown whether the fatally injured motorcyclist was wearing a helmet in 12 of the motorcycle crashes.

The highest number of injuries occurred in the 41- to 60-year-old age group. As might be expected, the lowest percentage of injuries occurred in the 15-and-under and 71-and-over age groups. Deaths occurred most frequently among riders in the 51 to 55-year-old age range, with 56 to 60-year-olds having the second highest number of fatalities.

The data show motorcycle drivers were determined to be "in error" about 55.2 percent of the time. Non-motorcycle drivers were determined to be in error 35.4 percent of the time. Animals were responsible for two motorcycle crashes, and the causes of the remaining crashes were "not determined." Of the 134 fatal crashes, motorcyclists were found to be in error 85 times, or about 63 percent of the time.

In reviewing crash statistics and working with other traffic safety facilities, Ohio has developed a program called "Motorcycle Ohio," which offers motorcycle rider training courses at various sites throughout Ohio.

A "Motorcycle Accident Factors" study was conducted by the Traffic Safety Center of the University of Southern California, which researched 1,100 crashes over a two-year period. The study found:

- More than half of riders who crashed had fewer than five months' experience on their motorcycles;

- Crashes involved motorcyclists who did not have a motorcycle license, or any license, or had had their licenses revoked;

- Untrained motorcyclists often do not understand and have not practiced how to use motorcycle brakes;

- Untrained riders often do not understand how to counter-steer and steer their motorcycle into an object they are trying to avoid;

- Almost half of the fatal motorcycle accidents indicated alcohol involvement;

- Motorcyclist errors were the primary cause of accidents involving one vehicle;

- Helmeted riders and passengers showed significantly fewer head and neck injuries at all levels of injury severity.

The U.S. Department of Transportation's National Highway Transportation Safety Administration (NHTSA) has compiled data showing that a motorcyclist is 35 times more likely to be involved in a deadly accident than someone in a passenger car.

Additional causes of motorcycle crashes will be discussed in Chapter 3.

Chapter 2

Ohio Motorcycle Safety Laws

In Ohio, a motorcyclist is not required by law to wear a helmet unless he or she is under 18 years of age or holds a motorcycle operator's endorsement or license bearing a "novice" designation that is currently in effect. A motorcycle operator must also wear a helmet if he or she is driving with a valid temporary instruction permit. If the operator of the motorcycle is required to wear a helmet, any passenger must also wear one. These laws are codified in the Ohio Revised Code at R.C. 4511.53.

Only 19 states have universal helmet laws requiring all riders to wear helmets. Three states—Illinois, New Hampshire, and Iowa—have no helmet laws.

A motorcyclist's helmet and safety glasses (or other protective eye device) must conform to regulations promulgated by Ohio's Director of Public Safety. Eye protection is required in Ohio unless the bike is equipped with a windscreen.

Ohio law also prohibits a person operating a motorcycle from riding "other than upon . . . the permanent and regular seat attached thereto" or carrying any other person upon the motorcycle other than upon a firmly attached and regular seat.

A person may ride a motorcycle only while sitting "astride" the seat, facing forward with one leg on each side of the motorcycle. It is unlawful to carry more persons at one time than the number of people for which the motorcycle is designed and equipped.

A footrest and a passenger seat are required for any passenger. DMV.org, a privately owned website, cautions that carrying passengers can affect different aspects of a bike's handling and is not like carrying a heavy suitcase or a large package on the back of the bike. DMV.org is designed to assist drivers with issues relating to the various state motor vehicle departments. The organization recommends that motorcyclists practice carrying a passenger in a low-traffic area and consider taking a safety course before riding with passengers. There is no age restriction for motorcycle passengers in Ohio.

Ohio law does not restrict the use of helmet speakers, but earplug use is prohibited while driving a motorcycle.

Additional information about motorcycle equipment, whether Ohio accepts motorcycle endorsements from other states, and other issues concerning motorcycles can be obtained by visiting motorcycle.ohio.gov and dmv.org/oh-ohio/motorcycle-license.php.

Many practices concerning the safe operation of motorcycles are clearly defined, but there are exceptions. For example, there is disagreement whether "lane splitting" is dangerous or might make riding safer in certain situations. Lane splitting is the practice of a motorcycle passing between lanes of stopped or slowly moving traffic going in the same direction. The practice is legal in California and some foreign countries. Bills have been introduced to legalize lane splitting in various other states throughout the U.S., but none have been enacted.

The American Motorcycle Association (AMA) claims there is evidence that lane splitting slightly reduces rear-end crashes for motorcyclists and provides them with an escape route in some situations.

In Ohio, lane splitting is not specifically authorized by statute, but it is not expressly defined as illegal either. That does not mean, however, that a motorcyclist engaging in the practice won't be cited for failure to drive in marked lanes or engaging in an unsafe lane change.

Ohio law requires a motorcyclist to carry at least $25,000 in liability insurance to cover property damage, $25,000 in bodily injury insurance for an accident involving one person, and $50,000 in bodily injury insurance for an accident involving two or more persons. Other proof of financial responsibility is also permissible – such as obtaining a certificate issued by the BMV indicating that money or government bonds in the amount of $30,000 is on deposit with the office of the Treasurer of the State of Ohio. The penalty for not meeting the insurance and financial responsibility requirements is loss of driving privileges for up to two years.

More information about insurance can be found in Chapter 8.

A person seeking a motorcycle license must pass a written exam to secure a Temporary Instruction Permit Identification Card (TIPIC). He or she must then take a Basic Rider Course or a motorcycle skills test. Those seeking a motorcycle license are required to become familiar with Ohio's Motorcycle Operator's Manual and the Digest of Ohio Motor Vehicle Laws.

Chapter 3

Common Causes of Motorcycle Crashes

Motorcycle crashes do not necessarily occur more often than other types of vehicular collisions, but they are more likely to result in serious injury or death. According to the NHTSA, deaths from motorcycle crashes per mile traveled in 2012 were 26 times higher than deaths from auto crashes. In the vast majority of these crashes, cars strike motorcycles from the front—78 percent of the time.

The single most dangerous situation for motorcyclists is a car making a left-hand turn in front of them. This situation occurs in 42 percent of car-motorcycle collisions, according to NHTSA data. The turning car usually hits the motorcycle when the motorcycle is:

- Going straight through an intersection;
- Passing the car; or
- Trying to overtake the car.

Although this is also a common crash scenario for two automobiles, the smaller size of the motorcycle makes it less visible to the turning vehicle.

Lane splitting can also cause crashes because:

- The cars are in close proximity to the motorcycle;
- The motorcycle has reduced space in which to maneuver; and
- Car drivers may not anticipate the motorcycle will be passing them in stopped or slowed traffic.

About half of single motorcycle crashes are caused by speeding and alcohol use. These factors play a large role in other motorcycle crashes, as well. In 2010, the NHTSA reported 29 percent of fatal motorcycle crashes involved riders with a blood alcohol level above the .08 legal nationwide limit.

The Centers for Disease Control and Prevention (CDC) reported that alcohol-related motorcycle accidents were on the increase with adults between the ages of 40 and 44, but young adults, ages 20 to 24, still lead as the age group with the most alcohol-related motorcycle crashes.

Close to half of all motorcycle crashes do not involve another vehicle. The rider collides with a fixed object, and speeding is often the main factor in these crashes. According to the NHTSA, 35 percent of all fatal crashes in 2008 were the result of speeding. Additionally, speeding motorcyclists who are not wearing protective gear, such as a helmet, more than double their risk of being killed in a crash.

The Ohio Department of Public Safety's data reflects that 91 of the 140 motorcyclists killed in 2014 (65 percent) were not wearing a helmet. Motorcycles provide little protection to the driver or passenger, unlike a car which shields the person inside by encasing them in a box of metal. Serious injury or death is, therefore, more likely in a motorcycle crash.

Road hazards pose another danger for motorcyclists. Potholes, dead animals, slick pavements, uneven lanes, and insufficient signs or warnings on roadways may all contribute to motorcycle crashes as well.

It has also been shown that high-performance motorcycles, such as "supersport" or "sport" motorcycles, are more likely to be involved in fatal crashes. The death rate of supersport riders is four times that of other motorcycle riders.

A supersport motorcycle is a motorcycle built on a racing platform that is modified for highway use. Supersport bikes are lightweight and have high horsepower engines that can go extremely fast— sometimes as fast as 160 mph. Sport bikes are similar but have a lower power-to-weight ratio. Statistics show the drivers of these types of motorcycles are generally 34 years old or younger.

Chapter 4

Common Injuries in Motorcycle Crashes

According to the Centers for Disease Control and Prevention (CDC), "[m]otorcycle deaths and injuries are an important public health concern and economic liability in the United States." Citing NHTSA data, the CDC reported that motorcycle-related deaths have increased by 55 percent since 2000 and that "[t]he economic burden from crash-related injuries and deaths in one year alone totaled $12 billion." Included in these dollar amounts are substantial costs that injured motorcyclists and their families must bear after a collision.

Traumatic Brain Injury

According to the NHTSA, traumatic brain injury (TBI) is the leading cause of death in motorcycle crashes. At a recent panel of brain surgeons in Akron, Ohio, the surgeons said the best way to avoid TBI is to wear a helmet. The NHTSA reports use of a helmet reduces the risk of death by 37 percent for motorcycle drivers and 41 percent for motorcycle passengers. The CDC reports that helmets reduce the risk of head injury by 69 percent.

TBI is a traumatically induced structural injury and/or physiological disruption of brain function as a result of head trauma. A direct blow to the head is not necessary, as is the case in a motor vehicle crash where one's head is thrown forward or backward with great force – so-called "whiplash."

TBI occurs on a microscopic level within the brain. The brain is normally covered with and protected by cerebral spinal fluid, which prevents it from striking the inside of a person's skull and suffering injury. Sometimes the fluid is not enough to protect the brain during a trauma, and the brain impacts with the rough portions of a person's skull, damaging or destroying millions of brain cells in an instant. This is referred to as "shearing."

The terms "mild" or "moderate" TBI refer to the degree and length of loss of consciousness, and not the severity of damage to brain function. A concussion is generally considered a mild form of TBI. Even mild TBI can have severe consequences and may result in permanent and total disability. The severity of symptoms may increase if the injured person has suffered previous concussions.

Even if a person thinks he or she is not injured, any blow to the head is a reason to seek medical attention. Symptoms can worsen over time, and what initially seems to be a minor injury, could become major.

Neck and Spinal Cord Injuries

Neck and spinal cord injuries are very common in motorcycle crashes. According to the American Academy of Orthopedic Surgeons, "[n]eck pain may result from abnormalities in the soft tissues—the muscles, ligaments, and nerves—as well as in bones and disks of the spine." Neck injuries may be the source of pain in other areas of the body as well, including pain in the upper back, shoulders, or arms. Neck injuries can be severe and even result in paralysis, requiring long-term assisted care.

Anyone who has injuries to the neck, back, or spine should seek immediate medical care, especially if he or she is experiencing continuous and persistent pain, severe pain, pain or numbness radiating into the arms or legs, or weakness of the arms or legs.

Road Rash

Road Rash is the most common injury in motorcycle crashes. It happens when exposed skin contacts the pavement. Sometimes thinner clothing can be scraped away by the impact of the rider on gravel or other rough surfaces. Road rash can be more than just cuts and bruises. If the skin is not properly treated, the motorcyclist could suffer permanent nerve damage, skin infections, or permanent irritations.

Protective clothing and equipment such as kneepads, gloves, jeans, and jackets may help prevent road rash.

Fractures

Motorcycle crashes can also result fractured bones. According to the CDC, motorcyclists commonly fracture bones of the legs and feet, face, upper trunk such as the ribs or sternum, arms and hands, and lower trunk such as the pelvis.

Sometimes these injuries are disabling. The presence of road rash can complicate fracture injuries as well.

Biker's Arm

This injury is caused by damage to the nerves in the upper arm suffered during a fall. A biker may instinctively draw his or her arms around or in front of himself or herself to lessen the impact. Permanent damage and even paralysis may occur. Protective clothing—such as jackets and elbow pads—can help lessen or prevent "biker's arm."

Traumatic Disfigurement, Amputations

Motorcycle crashes can also result in the loss or permanent disfigurement of a body part. Crash victims sometimes suffer burn injuries or come in contact with metal that severs a limb. Other injuries can result in serious scarring or necessitate amputations. While the use of a helmet and other protective gear certainly decreases the risk of serious injury, it cannot ensure that a motorcyclist will survive a crash unscathed.

Chapter 5

What to Do after a Motorcycle Crash

Gather Pertinent Information Before Discussing Fault

Ohio law requires motorists to share insurance and driver's license information. But you have the right to refuse to talk or give a statement to the insurance adjuster representing the other driver. You also have the right to refuse to sign any medical authorization forms requested by the other driver's insurance carrier. These forms will often give the insurance company broad access to your private medical information, even if it is unrelated to the crash, and it may later be used to deny your claim.

It is generally advisable to exercise these rights until you have had an opportunity to speak with an attorney. Premature statements about the cause of the crash, your injuries, or whether you are under the care of a doctor may later be used against you. Make statements only to the police and paramedics. Do not move your motorcycle unless it is dangerous for it to remain where it sits. If you leave things as they were when the crash occurred, this will give authorities a more accurate picture of what truly happened.

Generally, you will need to notify your insurance carrier about the crash, but be careful about making any statements concerning fault. Your ability to recover for your injuries may be compromised if you are too quick to take responsibility for something that may not turn out to be your fault, or may only partially be your fault, once all of the facts are learned. You should investigate the details of the crash and gather all pertinent information before making any determination about liability. That is what the insurance companies will do, and so should you.

Watch for Signs of Injury, Even if You Think You Are Okay Initially

Some injuries take time to reveal themselves, or their symptoms are misinterpreted as unrelated to the crash. For example, nausea and dizziness are often associated with a head injury, but people experience such symptoms in their everyday lives as well.

According to the VA/DoD Clinical Practice Guideline for Management of Concussion/"mTBI," a TBI victim will experience a new onset of worsening of at least one of the following symptoms immediately after the trauma:

• Any period of loss of or a decreased level of consciousness;

• Any loss of memory for events immediately before or after the injury (post-traumatic amnesia, or "PTA");

• Any alteration in mental state at the time of the injury;

• Neurological deficits (e.g., weakness, balance disturbance, praxis, paresis/plegia, change in vision, aphasia, or other sensory alterations);

• Intracranial lesion.

Other symptoms of acute TBI include slurred speech, repeated nausea or vomiting, headache, blurred vision, ringing in the ear, bad taste in the mouth, loss of coordination, dizziness/lightheadedness. TBI can be mild, moderate, or severe, depending on injury characteristics.

Furthermore, symptoms believed to be associated with a benign soft tissue injury may end up lingering for months and turn out to be related to something more serious – like a spinal disc herniation. Just as it makes good sense to evaluate all available information before making any determinations about fault, it is also generally a good idea to give yourself some time to fully evaluate your health before making any assumption about the nature of your medical condition.

Consult with an Attorney

Again, it is prudent to gain as much information as possible before deciding how to proceed with your claim. Many attorneys offer free consultations. This means you can have the attorney review the facts of your case and offer free advice about your legal rights and how your claim should be handled. You should take advantage of the free information before deciding how to proceed.

Insurance carriers are well-versed in finding ways to minimize the amounts they have to pay you. If you have serious injuries, you should have an attorney represent you in the dealings with the at-fault driver's insurance company and, should it become necessary, a lawsuit to recover for your damages. The question of whether you should hire a lawyer to represent you is discussed further in Chapter 10.

Chapter 6

Motorcycle Safety

Licensure

Persons seeking a motorcycle license in Ohio must first pass a written examination entitling them to a temporary permit. They are then required to either complete an ODPS Basic Rider Course or take a motorcycle skills test. For those opting to take the Basic Rider Course, ODPS offers two options. The first option is the standard Basic Rider Course (BRC). It is a 16-hour course designed for new riders and includes both classroom instruction and practice riding sessions. The second option is the Basic Rider Course for Returning Riders (BRC-RR), which is shorter course designed for more experienced riders. Visit the website, www.motorycle.ohio.gov, for more information and to register.

Helmets

In Ohio, the motorcyclists are not required to wear a helmet unless they are under 18 years of age, have a temporary permit, or are novice riders. Novice riders are riders who have had their motorcycle endorsement for less than one year. If the motorcycle operator is required to wear a helmet, so is the passenger. Of the 140 motorcyclists killed in Ohio in 2014, 91 were not wearing a helmet.

Visibility

Visibility is another hazard faced by motorcyclists. A motorcycle's narrow profile can make it harder to see than other vehicles on the road. Wearing bright colors helps to make a motorcyclist more visible to other motorists.

In the same vein, motorcyclists should always have their headlights on. A motorcycle with its headlights on is twice as likely to be seen. Headlight modulators can vary the intensity of the light during the day, making the motorcycle even more visible. It is also a good idea to flash your brake lights before slowing down, especially if a motorist is traveling too closely. Reflectors, reflective tape, decals, and custom light kits all make a motorcycle more visible as well, especially at night.

Common Motorcycle Accidents

Authors of the website, Rideapart.com, have prepared a list of "10 Common Motorcycle Accidents" with suggestions on how to avoid them. Wes Siler, author of the article, offers these tips: (For more complete information, consult the Rideapart.com website.)

1. A car turns left in front of you.

This is the most common crash scenario. The car driver "fails to see you or judges your speed incorrectly, turning in front of you at an intersection. Blame inattention, distraction, blind spots and even psychology; a driver looking for cars perceives merely an absence of cars, not the presence of a motorcycle."

To avoid the crash, you need to see it coming. Siler suggests developing a sort of "sixth sense." Anticipate unseen hazards and the potential that another motorist may turn in front of you. Pay close attention to cars stopped in traffic waiting to turn, and watch for gaps in traffic near intersections, driveways, and parking lots.

Observe the wheels of cars, as opposed to the cars themselves. The wheels will give you the first clue of movement and the direction the driver plans to travel. Be aware of what is behind you and to your sides so that you can take evasive action if necessary. Always have an escape route planned. Pay attention to the road surface, as well. Is it able to handle the full force of your brakes? Your best chance of survival, according to Siler, is to shed speed pre-collision. Do not lock your brakes or lay your bike down. Keep the bike upright. Use both brakes to reduce your speed as much as possible. "Even if you only have time to lose 10 or 20mph, that could be the difference between going home with bruises and [not] going home at all."

2. You hit loose material on the road.

Loose material, such as sand, gravel, leaves, etc., poses a hazard for motorcyclists, especially when a rider is leaning into a turn or applying his brakes. Obviously, avoiding the hazard altogether is most preferable. Siler recommends riding at a pace where your reaction time and ability to take action fit within your range of vision. Enter a corner wide at an easy pace to increase your field of vision. Pick up speed on the way out of the turn after you have seen your way through.

He also suggests learning more advanced techniques such as trail braking and using the full width of the road to maximize your vision.

3. You enter a corner too fast.

Motorcyclists entering a corner too fast can find themselves riding off of the roadway or unintentionally crashing into another vehicle or a stationary object.

It is important to ride only as fast as you can see. Use visual clues such as telephone poles and signs to judge a road's direction, even if the roadway cannot be seen over a crest. If you find yourself going too fast around a corner, Siler suggests taking as much of a lean as you can and trusting the bike to ride it out. Do not make any abrupt adjustments that could cause a loss of traction, such as hammering on the brakes or chopping the throttle. Again, he recommends learning trail braking skills to help you safely shed speed while already in the corner.

4. A car changes lanes into you.

Unfortunately, drivers looking for cars aren't programmed to look for motorcycles. You need to be aware of blind spots and try to stay out of them. If you can see a driver's eyes in his or her mirror, the driver can see you. If traffic slows and one lane is moving fast, drivers will want to be in that lane. Don't be there.

Be aware of turn signals, wheels turning, drivers moving their heads, drivers checking their mirrors, etc. In other words, be aware and always be looking for clues of impending danger.

5. A car rear-ends you.

Siler warns that what would be a rear-end fender bender between two cars "can kill a motorcyclist." When stopping in traffic, try to find what Siler calls a "crumple zone" by pulling in front of cars stopped ahead. This will create a "cushion" between you and any impact that might occur behind you. If this is not an option, stop to the side of the lane, rather than in the center. Keep the motorcycle in gear, and be prepared to scoot away if necessary, even if it means using the berm to pull around stopped traffic. You can also make yourself more visible to traffic behind you by tapping your brake lever.

6. A motorcyclist riding in your group runs into you.

When riding in a group, make sure everyone knows riding etiquette and understands how to ride in staggered formation. "Doing so increases vision and moves bikes out of line with each other, meaning a temporary lapse in attention won't result in a collision."

7. You lock your front brake.

The front brake generally supplies about 70 to 90 percent of a motorcycle's stopping power. Applying too much pressure to the brake handle, however, can lock the brake and lead to a crash.

The obvious solution is to learn how to brake properly. Siler suggests practicing in an open parking lot to learn how much force you can apply to your brakes without skidding. The rider needs to brake to the threshold of skidding, but not skid. The goal is to maximize traction. Skidding is a loss of traction that results from the buildup of heat as the locked tire slides across the ground, which increases stopping distance.

If you purchase a motorcycle with an anti-lock brake system (ABS), you won't have to worry about accidentally locking your brakes. ABS automatically prevents uncontrolled skidding – no matter how hard you pull on the brake lever.

8. A motorist opens a car door in front of you.

Be aware of the hazard posed by parked cars. Pedestrians walk between parked cars, cars pull out in to traffic, and people open their car doors as you ride by. It is, therefore, not a good idea to ride between an active traffic lane and parked cars. But if someone does open a car door in front of you, brake as hard as possible – without causing your motorcycle to skid. The more speed you shed before impact, the greater the likelihood you will not suffer serious injury.

9. You get stuck riding in the rain unprepared.

Rain can be treacherous for riders. You may head out on a sunny day only to find yourself miles from home with gray rain clouds rolling in. If you end up having to ride in the rain, it is important to remember some of the following points.

Rain reduces traction by reducing contact with the road and preventing your tires from adequately warming up. Rain also has a tendency to cause accumulated dirt and oils to form a slippery film on the road. Thus, you should make sure your tires are safe for wet conditions, with plenty of sipes in the tread and "tacky" rubber.

Although motorcycle tires are less likely to hydroplane than car tires, it can happen. Wider tires and faster speeds increase the risk of hydroplaning. Make sure you have plenty of tread on your tires to displace the water and keep the rubber of your tire on the road.

Jeff Cobb of motorcycle.com suggests testing your traction by "carefully and very briefly us[ing] the rear brake to the point of lock-up. This works in the dry too, and is a better-than-nothing gauge based on how easily your tire breaks loose. Do it on a flat part of the road – not on a crowned or cambered section, because the wheel will follow gravity and go out of line."

Watch for metal grates, metal plates, manhole covers, and railroad tracks, which, when hit at an angle, can steer your front wheel and instantly cause you to crash. Painted lines and crosswalks can be slippery too, especially if you are turning right or left and hit the line at an angle. Slow down more than usual, and take the turn riding straight up, rather than in a lean.

Going up a gear can help prevent spinning your tires on the roadway.

Weather conditions can also create limited visibility that calls for earlier braking and longer following distances.

10. You choose to drink and ride.

According to Traffic Safety Facts compiled by the NHTSA for 2013, 27 percent of motorcyclists involved in fatal crashes had a blood-alcohol content of .08 percent or higher. Citing a 1981 study known as the Hurt Report, Siler states that "alcohol is a factor in 50 percent of all bike wrecks."

There is no reason to add this risk to riding dangers, not to mention the penalties the state imposes on drunk drivers.

Chapter 7

What Compensation am I Entitled to Recover If Injured in a Motorcycle Crash?

Compensatory Damages

A motorcyclist who suffers injury due to another's carelessness is entitled to recover compensatory damages. Compensatory damages include both economic damages and non-economic damages. Economic damages include out-of-pocket costs like medical expenses, loss of wages, and loss of property—things easy to assign a dollar value to.

Non-economic damages include pain and suffering, inconvenience, physical impairment, disfigurement, and other non-pecuniary injury. For example, the mental and emotional trauma of having experienced the crash and the resultant physical pain and having to deal with that pain, having to go through surgery, or having to avoid certain activities would all be considered non-economic damages. These types of damages are less tangible and can be difficult to prove to insurance adjusters or juries.

To recover for pain and suffering in Ohio, the victim must prove he or she suffered some amount of economic loss. The Ohio Legislature has set "caps" on pain and suffering awards, setting maximum dollar amounts that an injured party may recover.

Punitive damages may also be available when there has been extreme negligence or malicious action. Punitives are intended to punish and deter similar future behavior.

Comparative Fault

Even if the motorcyclist is partially at fault, he or she may be entitled to compensation.

Ohio has comparative negligence laws. If the motorcyclist is 51 percent or more at fault, he or she cannot recover any damages from the other at-fault party. If, however, the motorcyclist is less than 51 percent at fault, he or she receives compensation in proportion to the negligent party's percentage of fault. Do not let the fact that you may be partially at fault deter you from consulting with an attorney about your rights.

Injured Passengers

If a passenger is injured in a motorcycle crash, he or she has the same rights to compensation for personal injury as the driver of the motorcycle. So if the motorcycle driver has a right of recovery against another motorist for his or her negligence, so does the driver's passenger. And if the motorcycle driver is at fault or partially at fault – perhaps, he was operating the motorcycle in a reckless manner – the passenger may have right to recover from the motorcycle driver as well.

Do you have a claim, and what's it worth?

Whether you have a claim is tied to two critical questions: (1) is the other person liable; and (2) if so, how much is the other person's insurance company responsible to pay?

Answering the first question can sometimes be simple; other times it can be complicated. It all depends on the particular factual circumstances of your case. Whether the opposing party is liable can sometimes be a matter of common sense. Other times it requires significant legal analysis, investigation, and, potentially, hiring experts such as an accident reconstructionist.

The second question is generally not easy to answer and leads to significant disagreement between the parties. Insurance adjusters often-times have difficulty assigning value to a person's non-economic damages. Further, economic damages are often disputed. In Ohio, an injured person is entitled to recover the reasonable and necessary expenses arising from his or her injury. Medical bills are presumed to be reasonable, but the bills themselves do not necessarily establish the value of the treatment.

The opposing party will likely dispute the value of your medical bills by introducing evidence that the provider accepted less than the billed amount. Medical providers often "write off" or adjust a portion of their bills when health insurance payments are received. The opposing party will typically argue that the amount accepted to satisfy the bill is the reasonable value of the medical services, as opposed to the billed amount. The billed amount and the amount accepted to satisfy the bill can vary drastically.

There can be a significant difference between what the at-fault party or his insurance company wants to pay and what your attorney thinks the case is worth. Things are not always "cut-and-dried," and you need to be prepared for this.

You also need to keep in mind that statutes of limitations (deadlines for filing a lawsuit) apply to your claims. A negligence claim must generally be commenced within two years after the cause of action accrues. Other statutes of limitations may apply as well. For this reason, it is generally a good idea to proceed with claims soon after they arise. If the applicable statute of limitations dates come and go, you will be forever barred from filing a lawsuit.

Subrogation

Another issue that may affect your claim is "subrogation." Subrogation provides a party (usually your health insurance company) the right to stand in your shoes and proceed against the negligent person as if it was the owner of your injury claim. It permits your health insurer to recover the amounts it paid for your medical treatment out of compensation for your damages. Your health insurance company may also have a right of reimbursement from you directly if you obtain a recovery from the negligent party. This is sometimes referred to as a "lien" against your injury claim.

As one might suspect, problems arise when amounts demanded by your health insurance exceed amounts available under the negligent party's liability insurance. For example, assume the other motorist has $100,000 in coverage. Your injuries were significant and necessitated multiple surgeries and in-patient rehabilitation. You can no longer perform your very physical job duties as a carpenter. The associated medical payments from your health insurer were $150,000, and it is demanding all $100,000 from the other party's insurance company – leaving you with nothing to help with your ongoing treatment and the reduction of income you will suffer now and into the future. This may seem very unfair, but it can happen. There are legal arguments you can sometimes make to get your health insurance to reduce its lien amount.

You can probably see that you may need legal assistance with these issues. They can be complicated and difficult to navigate.

Wrongful Death

In a worst-case scenario, a motorcycle crash may involve a death, forcing the deceased person's estate to file a wrongful death lawsuit to recover damages.

'Wrongful death" in Ohio is governed by Chapter 2125 of the Ohio Revised Code and is defined as a death that is caused by "wrongful act, neglect, or default" of another. A wrongful death claim may be filed if the wrongful conduct "would have entitled the party injured to maintain an action and recover damages if death had not ensued."

Under Ohio law, the executor or appointed administrator of the deceased person's estate is the only person who can file a wrongful death action on behalf of the deceased's surviving beneficiaries, such as the deceased's spouse, parents, children, siblings, or grandparents.

The estate is permitted to recover a number of different types of damages, including:

(1) Loss of support (based upon the compensation the deceased person would have earned if he or she had lived);

(2) Loss of the services the deceased person would have performed;

(3) Loss of the care, companionship, advice, guidance, counsel, instruction, or society of the deceased person;

(4) Loss of the prospective inheritance of the deceased person's spouse or children;

(5) Mental anguish suffered by the surviving family members as a result of the untimely death.

The estate may also be entitled recover damages for the deceased person's conscious pain and suffering prior to death, the value of the medical expenses that were incurred prior to death, and reasonable funeral and burial expenses.

The statute of limitations for a wrongful death claim is two years. In other words, the claim must be filed within two years of the death.

Chapter 8

What about Insurance Coverage?

Liability Coverage

In Ohio, it is illegal to operate a "motor vehicle" without insurance or other proof of financial responsibility. A motorcycle is considered a motor vehicle.

A motorcycle insurance policy may include different types of coverage. One type of coverage is "liability" coverage. If you are at fault for the collision, liability coverage pays on your behalf for another's property damage and injuries.

Collision Coverage

You may also purchase "collision" or "physical damage" coverage, which will pay to repair or replace your motorcycle in the event of a collision (regardless of who was at fault).

Many banks will require you to carry this type of coverage in exchange for lending you money to purchase a motorcycle.

As discussed in Chapter 2, Ohio law may, under some circumstances, permit you to ride without a helmet. However, you should check with your insurance company to see whether coverage is conditioned upon wearing a helmet.

You may wonder whether your insurance policy covers you while riding another person's motorcycle or whether it covers a friend riding your motorcycle. Your agent should be able to answer these types of questions for you.

Medical Payments Coverage

Medical payments insurance ("MedPay") provides benefits to cover your or your passenger's collision-related medical expenses. This type of coverage applies no matter who is at fault and may provide coverage if you – and sometimes even if your family member – was a passenger on someone else's motorcycle.

MedPay is limited to a specific dollar amount and time period. Many policies limit coverage to medical treatment received within the first three years after a crash. In some cases, it applies only after medical insurance has reached its limits. MedPay, unlike many other types of insurance, does not require you to pay a deductible or co-payments.

Uninsured/Underinsured Motorist Coverage

If you are involved in a crash with an at-fault motorist who isn't insured or doesn't have enough coverage, you will have to turn to uninsured/underinsured motorist ("UM/UIM") coverage.

Uninsured motorist coverage protects you if the at-fault driver doesn't carry liability insurance. Underinsured motorist coverage, on the other hand, pays to the extent your coverage limits exceed the amount of the at-fault party's insurance limits.

Check with your insurance agent to see whether you have adequate coverage for these eventualities.

Sufficient limits

In Ohio, motorists are required to carry a minimum amount of liability insurance (property damage limits of $25,000 and bodily injury limits of $25,000 per person/$50,000 per accident). Additional coverage is at the option of the motorist.

Keep in mind that crashes may result in damages that exceed minimum coverage limits. If the at-fault driver's insurance policy limits are insufficient, the at-fault driver may be personally responsible to pay the deficiency.

Bad faith of insurance company

Your insurance company owes you a duty of good faith. Therefore, it must handle and process your claim with reasonable justification. This includes a duty to promptly and reasonably investigate claims. "Bad faith" occurs when your insurer violates its duty of good faith. The violation gives rise to an independent claim that may include compensatory damages, attorneys' fees, litigation costs, damages for emotional distress, prejudgment interest, and punitive damages if the insurer acted with malice.

Chapter 9

Will They Blame Me for My Injuries If I Was Not Wearing a Helmet?

Nearly 40 years ago, the federal government required states to enact motorcycle helmet laws to qualify for federal highway and safety funding. Most complied, and by the early 1970's, almost all states had universal helmet laws.

Since then, following a strong lobbying effort, Congress eliminated sanctions for failure to enact universal helmet use laws. As a result, 28 states, including Ohio, repealed or amended their helmet laws to permit certain motorcyclists to ride without helmets. Three states have no helmet laws whatsoever.

The NHTSA reports in states requiring universal helmet use, 86 percent of riders wear them. In states that don't require universal helmet use, 55 percent of motorcyclists wear them. In 2010, an NHTSA report showed motorcycle deaths had increased more than 100 percent during the previous 10 years. Motorcyclists have also noticed large increases in insurance requirements—up to $200,000 in medical coverage—when helmet laws are relaxed.

Injuries sustained while not wearing a helmet, especially head injuries, can complicate a motorcyclist's claim. As discussed in Chapter 7, comparative fault laws prohibit recovery if the motorcyclist is determined to be 51 percent or more at fault. If, however, he is less than 51 percent at fault, he will receive compensation in proportion to the other responsible party's percentage of fault.

Thus, the person who caused the collision – along with his or her insurance carrier – will likely attempt to make a motorcycle "helmet defense." They will argue that the motorcyclist was, at least, partially responsible for his or her injuries because he or she was not wearing a helmet.

Whether the motorcyclist's decision to not wear a helmet is negligence is an unsettled issue in Ohio.

In a case dating back to 1971 concerning the failure to wear a seatbelt, the Second District Court of Appeals held "there is no duty to anticipate another's negligence and to protect one's safety by wearing a safety device." *Roberts v. Bohn*, 26 Ohio App.2d 50 (1971). While this statement of law would, at first blush, appear to protect an injured motorcyclist from a helmet defense, the law is not so clear.

In a more recent decision from the Cuyahoga County Court of Common Pleas, the court determined that it was up to the jury to weigh the evidence and decide whether the decision not to wear a helmet was reasonable under the circumstances. *(See Rodriguez v. Cohen*, Cuyahoga County C.P. Case No. CV 09 700949 (Aug. 15, 2011.) Specifically, the court decided that the jury must determine 1) whether a reasonable person exercising ordinary care would have worn a helmet to avoid or lessen injury in the event of an accident, and, if so,

2) whether there is competent evidence establishing a causal connection between the motorcyclist's failure to wear a helmet and the injuries sustained.

The Second and Third District Courts of Appeals have upheld trial court decisions refusing to permit defendants to point their fingers at motorcyclists when there is no evidence that use of a helmet would have prevented or reduced the motorcyclist's injuries (*See Smiley v. Leonard,* 2nd Dist. No. 14071 (Feb. 16, 1994); *Kiefer v. Emery,* 3rd Dist. No. 17-94-19 (April 5, 1995).)

Because the Ohio Supreme Court has yet to consider this issue, the helmet defense will most certainly be something you will have to contend with if you are injured while not wearing a helmet.

Chapter 10

Do I Need a Lawyer?

Ohio law does not require you to hire a lawyer to pursue your personal injury claim. But that does not mean it is wise to proceed without one. Even the simplest case has its difficulties and challenges.

Within days, you may be contacted by insurance company representatives to obtain information regarding the crash and your injuries. Insurance representatives may even attempt to discuss settlement at that time – before you have a good grasp of what your medical condition is. In order to fully protect your rights, you should speak with an attorney before discussing the crash or your injuries with insurance representatives.

Insurance companies know how to defeat and minimize claims. They will work to protect their interests from the start, and it is generally a good idea to have a lawyer protecting your interests as well. Of course, the more serious your injuries are, the more important it is to have legal representation.

Other complicating factors may exist. For example, your health insurance providers may allege a "lien" against your injury claim, demanding the right to be repaid out of your claim for crash-related expenditures the insurers made on your behalf. Lien holders must meet certain legal requirements to prove their liens. And even assuming they do, you may have a right to a reduction of the lien amount. In other words, measures can be taken to protect your claim-related funds from third parties. Again, a competent injury attorney can help you navigate these issues.

Dealing with the aftermath of a motorcycle crash can be very stressful. On top of the emotional turmoil, physical pain, and disruption in your life, you have to deal with your property damage, medical treatment, the insurance companies, lien holders, legal issues, and a host of other matters.

A motorcycle injury lawyer can help alleviate these burdens so you can focus on what is most important – your recovery and getting back to living your life. A lawyer can also help level the playing field as you contend with well-financed insurance companies seeking to minimize your claim.

The Authors

The Ohio law firm of Slater & Zurz LLP is a team of legal professionals dedicated to helping victims of all types of accidents and their families throughout Ohio. The law firm has been entrusted to handle more than 30,000 personal injury cases and has helped clients receive in excess of $150 million in settlements and verdicts.

Attorney Jim Slater is the managing partner of Slater & Zurz LLP and has been actively practicing law for over 40 years. When Mr. Slater is asked what the law firm of Slater & Zurz LLP does, he replies simply by saying:

We Make Others Do What They Do Not Want To Do.

We make the decision makers at insurance companies pay fair and proper compensation to victims of accidents.

We make individuals and businesses pay their customers and employees the money they owe them.

We provide comfort to families by financially punishing owners of nursing homes that harm their loved ones.

We convince juries to award our clients the money they deserve.

In all cases, we work tirelessly to be sure our clients get what they are entitled to receive.

Prior to asking for our help, our clients were either denied proper compensation or were uncertain whether they could receive the compensation they deserved.

We have made companies pay millions when they negligently manufactured products that caused serious injuries.

We have made insurance companies pay hundreds of thousands of dollars when the dogs of homeowners they insured attacked innocent children and caused serious injury.

We have made a hospital pay millions when one of its doctors caused a child's death.

We made a large company pay millions to its employees when the company failed to pay commission income they earned.

At Slater & Zurz LLP all cases do not involve millions or hundreds of thousands of dollars. Many of our cases involve smaller amounts of money. But there is a common theme. We make companies and people who have treated or would treat our clients unfairly do what they do not want to do.

This is what we do at Slater & Zurz LLP. This is what we have done for over 30,000 clients over 40-plus years. I am personally proud of the difference we make for our clients. It has been our goal, from the beginning, to make people proud that we are their attorney and pleased with the results we obtain for them. This is what they tell us on a daily basis.

James W. Slater

Free Consultations Are Always Offered at

Slater & Zurz LLP

Akron • Canton • Cleveland • Columbus

Please call toll free

1-800-297-9191

or visit

slaterzurz.com

Other Useful and Informative Books by

Slater & Zurz LLP

When A Dog Bites

Fight Back

If you or someone you know becomes the victim of a dog attack in Ohio you have specific legal rights to take action. This book will help you understand your rights, how to file a dog bite claim and where you can turn for help to make sure you receive a fair amount for the injuries and damages you suffered.

To request your copy please call 1-800-297-9191 or visit our website focused on the needs of dog bite victims at **dogbitesohio.com**.

Stop Nursing Home Abuse in Ohio

To request your copy please call 1-800-297-9191 or visit our website focused on nursing home abuse and neglect in Ohio:

stopohionursinghomeabuse.com.

A Wrongful Death in Ohio

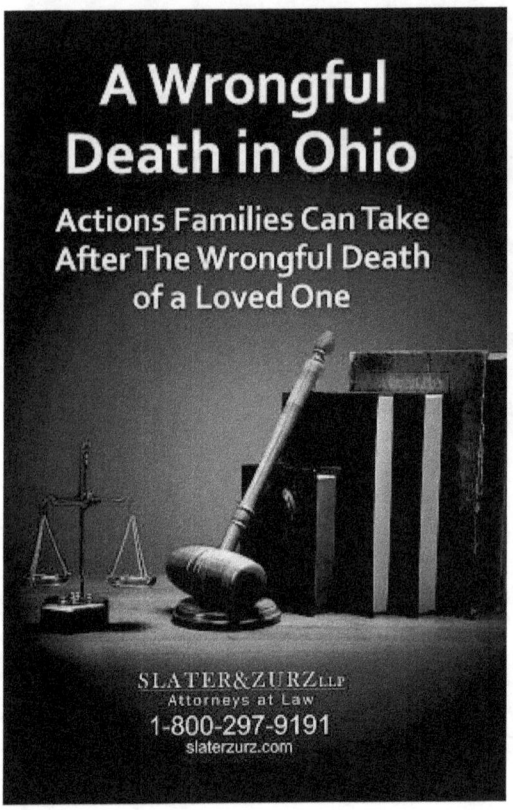

To request your copy please call 1-800-297-9191 or visit our website

focused on wrongful death in Ohio: **ohiowrongfuldeathlaw.com**

Legal Malpractice in Ohio

To request your copy please call 1-800-297-9191 or visit our website

focused on wrongful death in Ohio: ohiolegalmalpracticelaw.**com**

www.ingramcontent.com/pod-product-compliance
Lightning Source LLC
Chambersburg PA
CBHW071621170526
45166CB00003B/1137